ALSO BY FRANZ WRIGHT

Poetry

Tapping the White Cane of Solitude (1976)
The Earth Without You (1980)
8 Poems (1981)
The One Whose Eyes Open When You Close Your Eyes (1982)
Going North in Winter (1986)
Entry in an Unknown Hand (1989)
And Still the Hand Will Sleep in Its Glass Ship (1991)
Midnight Postscript (1992)
The Night World & the Word Night (1993)
Rorschach Test (1995)
Ill Lit: Selected & New Poems (1998)
Knell (1999)
God While Creating the Birds Sees Adam in His Thoughts (2001)
Hell & Other Poems (2001)
The Beforelife (2001)

Translations

Jarmila. Flies: Ten Prose Poems by Erica Pedretti (1976)
The Life of Mary (Poems by Rainer Maria Rilke) (1981)
The Unknown Rilke (1983)
No Siege Is Absolute (Poems by René Char) (1984)
The Unknown Rilke: Expanded Edition (1991)

WALKING
TO MARTHA'S VINEYARD

WALKING
TO MARTHA'S VINEYARD

Poems by

FRANZ WRIGHT

Alfred A. Knopf   *New York*   2004

THIS IS A BORZOI BOOK
PUBLISHED BY ALFRED A. KNOPF

Copyright © 2003 by Franz Wright

www.randomhouse.com/knopf/poetry

Knopf, Borzoi Books, and the colophon are
registered trademarks of Random House, Inc.

Library of Congress Cataloging-in-Publication Data
Wright, Franz, 1953–
Walking to Martha's Vineyard : poems / by Franz Wright.—1st ed.
        p.   cm.
ISBN 0-375-41518-1
I. Title.

PS3573.R5327W3 2003
811'.54—dc21   2002043375

Manufactured in the United States of America
Published October 17, 2003
Reprinted Twice
Fourth Printing, May 2004

Dieu créant les oiseaux voit Adam dans sa pensée

—Cathédrale de Chartres, Portail Nord

CONTENTS

Year One   3

On Earth   4

One Heart   5

Octaves   6

June Storm   7

The Word   8

The First Supper   10

Promise   11

Fathers   12

To John Wieners: Elegy & Response   14

Flight   16

Medjugorje   19

My Place   20

Study in Acid & Green   21

Antipsychotic   22

Old Story   23

Cloudless Snowfall   24

Shaving in the Dark   25

Registration of Names   27

5:00 Mass   28

Dudley Wright   29

University of One   30

Slip   31

Domesticity   32

Little Farm on the Ocean   33

Untitled ("She undressed . . .")   34

The Bird Bride   36

The Maker   37

Letter   38

Abandoned Letter   40

Saying   42

Baptism   44

April Orchard   46

Circle Drawn in Water   48

Weekend in the Underworld   50

Charlottesville Winter   51

Reunion   52

Auto-Lullaby   54

Childhood's Appointment   55

September Sunflower   57

P.S.   59

The Word "I"   60

How You Will Know Me   62

The New Jerusalem   63

Quest   64

Epitaph   65

The Poem   66

Diary Otherwise Empty   67

Icon From Childhood   68

The New Child   69

Walden   70

Walking to Martha's Vineyard   71

The Only Animal   73

Acknowledgments   77

WALKING
TO MARTHA'S VINEYARD

YEAR ONE

I was still standing
on a northern corner.

Moonlit winter clouds the color of the desperation of wolves.

Proof
of Your existence? There is nothing
but.

ON EARTH

Resurrection of the little apple tree outside
my window, leaf-
light of late
in the April
called her eyes, forget
forget—
but how
How does one go
about dying?
Who on earth
is going to teach me—
The world
is filled with people
who have never died

ONE HEART

It is late afternoon and I have just returned from
the longer version of my walk nobody knows
about. For the first time in nearly a month, and
everything changed. It is the end of March, once
more I have lived. This morning a young woman
described what it's like shooting coke with a baby
in your arms. The astonishing windy and altering light
and clouds and water were, at certain moments,
You.

There is only one heart in my body, have mercy
on me.

The brown leaves buried all winter creatureless feet
running over dead grass beginning to green, the first scent-
less violet here and there, returned, the first star noticed all
at once as one stands staring into the black water.

Thank You for letting me live for a little as one of the
sane; thank You for letting me know what this is
like. Thank You for letting me look at your frightening
blue sky without fear, and your terrible world without
terror, and your loveless psychotic and hopelessly
lost
    with this love

OCTAVES

We were, about as useful as a hammer and nail made of gold

Some woman crying the first thing we heard before our
        birth

No people anymore

Oh prayer of night

Who's going to miss you

JUNE STORM

Voices from the first dark heartshaped green of summer
leaves, rain;
birds'.

What are they called.

I'm leaving here, and still don't know.

I'm going there, though,
where they are—
I feel this.

Feel that I was there
before.

I felt this
as a child, and now
I know it.

THE WORD

Like a third set of teeth
or side in a chess match

Thought

and most mysterious
of all, the
matter of thought

The mortal mind thinking
deathless things,
singing

See it examining
black grains of death
and life—they are the same
thing—
in its open hand

Sweet black green-shadowed grains of soil:
When no one is looking

see it secretly

taste one.

THE FIRST SUPPER

Death, heaven, bread, breath and the sea
here

to scare me

But I too will be fed by
the other food
that I know nothing
of, the breath
the death
the sea of
    it

Day
when the almond does not
blossom and the grasshopper drags itself along

But if You can make a star from nothing You can raise me up

PROMISE

Long nights, short years. Forgiving
silence

When morning comes, and pain—

no one is a stranger, this whole world is your home.

FATHERS

Oh build a special city
for everyone who wishes

to die, where
they might help one another out

and never feel ashamed
maybe make a friend,

etc.
You

who created the stars and the sea
come down, come down

in spirit, fashion
a new heart

in me, create
me again—

Homeless in Manhattan
the winter of your dying

I didn't have a lot of time
to think about it, trying

to stay alive

To me

it was just the next interesting thing you would do—
that is how cold it was

and how often I walked to the edge of the actual
river to join you

TO JOHN WIENERS:
ELEGY & RESPONSE

The street outside
the window says
I don't miss you, and I don't wish you well

Says crocuses
coaxed out of hiding
and killed in the snow

Says six o'clock and a billion black birds
wheeling, and the dusk stars
wait, and the avalanche waits—

And have you looked at the paper today

Medical research discloses
that everyone is going to die
of something

Ulterior avenues, I will not take you

Supernaturally articulate pencil, where the heaven
of lost objects are you

Beginning summer now, incredibly close
clouds like an illustration
that disturbed you as a child

Appalling and incomprehensible mercy

The seeing see only this world

FLIGHT

I

That glass was it filled with alcohol, water, or light

At ten
I turned you into a religion

The solitary
four-foot priest of you, I kept
the little manger candle
burning, I
kept your black half-inch of
scripture
in the hiding place

Destroyer
of the world

That empty

glass

2

In which city was it, in fourth or fifth grade, Mother
read in the newspaper you'd be appearing

and dressed me up in suit
and little tie
and took me
I wanted to run to you—who were all these people?—
I sat alone beaming
at you who could not meet my eyes, and after
you shyly approached
and shook my hand

3

If I'm walking the streets of a city
covering every square inch of the continent
all its lights out
and empty of people,
even then
you are there

If I'm walking the streets
overwhelmed with this love for the living

I will still be a blizzard at sea

Since you left me at eight I have always been lonely

star-far from the person right next to me, but

closer to me than my bones you

you are there

4

It's 1963 again, the old Minneapolis airport so vast
        to me, and I am running
after the long flight alone I am running
into your huge arms—
Now
I am forty-five now and I am dreaming
we are together again we are both forty-five
and I have you all to myself this time, and we are walking
together we're walking down a glowing-blue tunnel
we're on time for our flight, I can hardly believe it
we are traveling somewhere together alone
God knows where we are going, and who cares
we're together, walking
and happily talking
and laughing, and breathing.

MEDJUGORJE

Highway shrine,
lighthouse
of time

in the bleached-
gold winter
wheat—

listening in
another tongue, I

walk there

Come help through
the long hour
of our death

MY PLACE
for Beth

Rain land, walnut blossoms raining
white
where I walk at sixteen

bright light in the north wind

Still sleeping bees at the grove's heart
(my heart's) till the sun
its "wake now"
kiss, the million
friendly gold huddlings
and burrowings of them hearing the shining
wind
I hear, my only
cure for the loneliness I go through:

more.

I believe one day the distance between myself and God will
disappear.

STUDY IN ACID & GREEN

On Broadway
blonde high-heeled skinny
kindersluts smoking and giggling
in terror

The dark side of the
knife

And the way certain places
on earth amount
to forgetting
the future,
        and heaven's
prefiguration—

Then the I died (for laughter and beauty)

ANTIPSYCHOTIC

The beating of her neighbor's heart
upstairs keeps her awake
all night

We don't learn
she thinks
we remember

If we're lucky

Now she is going to put on some
nice cut-your-wrists music

"Most of the poetry I read
makes me feel like I'm already dead"

And look everything is turning
into something else
(and that is true)

Risperdal whisperdoll

all alone in the dark
garden

blowing out a dandelion

OLD STORY

First the telephone went,
then
the electricity.

It was cold,
and they both went to sleep
as though dressed for a journey.

Like addictions condoned
from above evening
fell, lost

leaves waiting
to come back as leaves—
the long snowy divorce . . .

That narrow bed, a cross
between an altar
and an operating table. Voice

saying, While I was alive
I loved you.
And I love you now.

CLOUDLESS SNOWFALL

Great big flakes like white ashes
at nightfall descending
abruptly everywhere
and vanishing
in this hand like the host
on somebody's put-out tongue, she
turns the crucifix over
to me, still warm
from her touch two years later
and thank you,
I say all alone—
Vast *whisp-whisp* of wingbeats
awakens me and I look up
at a minute-long string of black geese
following low past the moon the white
course of the snow-covered river and
by the way thank You for
keeping Your face hidden, I
can hardly bear the beauty of this world.

SHAVING IN THE DARK

How old is the sun today

Where are the shoes of yesteryear

What an evil potato goes through
we can never know, but
I'm beginning to resemble one

Ah, a little light now

It is the hour
the moment
when it becomes possible
to distinguish a white
thread from a black,
so prayer begins

I see a shadowy reflection now our fingers touch

There's nothing like what is

fragile and momentary
as the pale yellow light along the windowsill
in winter north
of nowhere yet
if not for winter, nothing
would get done

would finally get done

I've been all around this world

and not to die in hell
not to die in the flames of hell homeless with a cell phone please

There's nothing like today

And contributing one's atoms to the green universe
how strange is that

And some have managed to live in a constant awareness
that all things, every evil thing
will be forgotten, neglecting
to mourn for every radiant thing, and so seeing
the radiance.

REGISTRATION OF NAMES

I see us in our late teens
beautiful and damaged
like the gene for mania, but more fun
than a topless rodeo
Ghosts

of the future, the young—
childhood plus sex
make one one
lunatic wanderer, in the midwestern autumn
solemn and Rimbaudian

Some plausibly sorrowful lie
got me into this, maybe
one will get me out

The decade began with the chaste knight,
and concluded with a visit

from General Franz P. Wright, supreme commander
of paranoid recluses, grayhaired
children, a weird page a day
a dark hilarity
awful to live without as love.

5:OO MASS

The church is a ship in the brightening snowstorm;

shafts of light falling in through blue windows.

It's almost night and starting to get light!

The planet, too, adrift

in an infinite blizzard of stars—

Where most of us are sick

and starving in the pitching dark, and the partying

masters up above

don't know where we are either.

We love one another. We don't really know

anyone well, but

we love one

another

DUDLEY WRIGHT

Lighting a candle for my father
I am also my father
lighting a candle

for *his*
in the past, where he is
also his father

lighting one for me

UNIVERSITY OF ONE

And I've lost my fear
of death
here, what death?
There is no such thing.
There is only
mine,
or yours—
but the world
will be filled with the living. Mysteriously
(heavy dear sky-colored book), too,
I have been spared
the fate of those who love words
more than what they mean!
My poem is not
for example
a blank check in pussyland
anymore,
nor
entry in the contest for the world's
most poignant suicide
note. Now
I have to go—, but
meet my friend Miss April
snow.

SLIP

The black balloon
tied to her wrist again, thin hand
floating
an inch above the white
white sheet

The body
a word to be said
into death, one
word
which no one else knows
completely her own—

Night just the shadow of her hell

DOMESTICITY

Gray small clumps weightless as hair dust what is it

Forty years later
utterly unrecognizable
save for our eyes

that is, were we to meet—

LITTLE FARM ON THE OCEAN

Take one by mouth
furtively
every four minutes

Dear miniature sky-

blue
antisacrament . . .

Goodbye

(and God have mercy on my monster)

UNTITLED

She undressed
looking into my eyes
like someone about to go swimming at dawn alone

quiet heart attack

Thirst is my water

Some say
the more you stray
the more you're
saved,

I wouldn't be surprised

Snow falling
on my bedclothes

Set the mind
before the mirror of eternity ,

and everything will work

THE BIRD BRIDE

Hangs from her neck
down her thin back a pouch
made from feathers
(doesn't say
what's inside it), the sacrificed
girl, the bird
bride I call her:
the child, the
Siberian blizzard
girl, the
mummy
of the snows. In the pouch
is the spring
the one
spring day, a hidden
word—her first
and last, *I*
say,
her name;
in the next column
monkeys stone herder to death
in eastern Kenya.

THE MAKER

Planet, the mind
said, *all*
poppyfield

as I was
waking—

The listening voice, the speaking ear

And the way, always, being
a maker
reminds:

you were made.

LETTER

January 1998

I am not acquainted with anyone
there, if they spoke to me
I would not know what to do.
But so far nobody has, I know
I certainly wouldn't.
I don't participate, I'm not allowed;
I just listen, and every morning
have a moment of such happiness, I breathe
and breathe until the terror returns. About the time
when they are supposed to greet one another
two people actually look into each other's eyes
and hold hands a moment, but
the church is so big and the few who are there
are seated far apart. So this presents no real problem.
I keep my eyes fixed on the great naked corpse, the vertical
    corpse
who is said to be love
and who spoke the world
into being, before coming here
to be tortured and executed by it.
I don't know what I am doing there. I do
notice the more I lose touch
with what I previously saw as my life
the more real my spot in the dark winter pew becomes—

it is infinite. What we experience
as space, the sky
that is, the sun, the stars
is intimate and rather small by comparison.
When I step outside the ugliness is so shattering
it has become dear to me, like a retarded
child, precious to me.
If only I could tell someone.
The humiliation I go through
when I think of my past
can only be described as grace.
We are created by being destroyed.

ABANDONED LETTER

Dear child, old

child

how I miss you
how I wish you
well

beautiful boy
reading
to yourself;

    your big *Iliad*
your *Green Lantern*
all the books

on dinosaurs and stars
the atom,

    glad
and learned
child

with the strange name

too sick
for your lost friends
to cry

every minute
of your hidden
devoted
and resourceful walking
day

   how I wish you were mine

you would never have to be lonely

those insane so-called parents
of ours

don't worry
I would take care of them—

SAYING

Sunlight of the spirit—

Courage is not the absence of fear

Word
of the four billion letters
whose spelling
determined the color
of my eyes
and my ultimate
fate, so they say

Rumi says, out beyond ideas
of doing good and doing evil
there is a field

I'll meet you there

I want one
good look at
Rodin's "The Shitter"

It is my intention God
damn it to ride
on the heights
of the earth, I have visited

every last
nook and cranny of the depths

You may find a dead bird you won't see
a flock of them
anywhere

BAPTISM

That insane asshole is dead
I drowned him
and he's not coming back. Look
he has a new life
a new name
now
which no one knows except
the one who gave it.

If he tastes
the wine now
as he is allowed to
it won't, I'm not saying it
will
turn to water

however, since You
can do anything, he
will be safe

his first breath as an infant
past the waters of birth
and his soul's, past the death waters, married—

Your words are spirit
and life.
Only say one
and he will be healed.

APRIL ORCHARD

We think if we're not conscious we exist
we won't exist, but
how can that be?
Just look at the sun.
Oh, if I could only make myself
completely unafraid—once
born, we never die—
what talks we'd have, and will. It's theorized
the universe is only one
among others, infinite
others. Though
didn't Christ tell us, "In my father's house
there are many rooms . . ."
And I would tell you
what it's like,
real fear. And
how there are human beings for whom the sun
is never going to shine
is never going to rise again, ever, not
really—
not the real sun.
They're not exactly waking up
in radiant awareness
and celebration of their own presence these days,
who'd get rid of themselves with no more thought

(if it were possible) than you would give to
taking off a glove.
How in deep sleep sometimes even we get well.
So you can believe me, in the far deeper
sleep (these new apple leaves, maybe) we are all going
to be perfectly all right.

CIRCLE DRAWN IN WATER

I think somewhere there is a room
in which I am living
an old man

in the future,
in a windy
room where I'm sitting and reading

trying to make out
bent over a three-legged table

these words I'm now writing—

in what will then be
passing for the present,
blindly

trying to read to remember
the room
the light the time of day
when I first set them down

What a pile of shit, I'll say

and What was her name
What the hell
was her name

I will slowly get up then
and walk to the window, this time

this place dear to me

even in the muteness

the absolute unsayableness
of the simplest thing in pain
the way it was, exactly
as it was
when I began

WEEKEND IN THE UNDERWORLD

Once I held your face
in my hands, I saw through
space

Poor spirit
drifting off now

like smoke in pouring rain

Wait—
are you there?

Everywhere. I'm

everywhere

CHARLOTTESVILLE WINTER

Tomorrow is history, lead singer of nothing;

unfurnished spirit, chair

selected from the curb—

little manual on

my desk, the oven door.

REUNION

Snow over the scarred fields just ending, between clouds
a candle in a horse skull
moon
at dawn—
My sin is always before me.

In the end the price of understanding
everything will be, of
its communication
to those who stand around you,
the complete and absolute
impossibility,
but

does this mean
I won't remember
Earth? Perhaps
it does, but
I don't know.
Soon I will find out.

       Snow over
the scarred fields
just ending,
what lies

before me is my past.
That is,

should I father a fatherless child.

March 18, 2001
Oberlin

AUTO-LULLABY

Think of a sheep
knitting a sweater;
think of your life
getting better and better.

Think of your cat
asleep in a tree;
think of that spot
where you once skinned your knee.

Think of a bird
that stands in your palm.
Try to remember
the Twenty-first Psalm.

Think of a big pink horse
galloping south;
think of a fly, and
close your mouth.

If you feel thirsty, then
drink from your cup.
The birds will keep singing
until they wake up.

CHILDHOOD'S APPOINTMENT

I am blind, but it seems to me the street meanders, it seems to
    wish itself to sea.

But we're climbing now, I have come to stand on a great height
     overlooking
the white city

silver mirror-glare of bay, of

the goodbye
against which nobody with pride would dare plead—

Here's hope you are well into your blessed summer

Cockroach befriended by the insane prisoner

At the wedding there weren't many guests

Visible ones, anyway

Then the beautiful hidden and infinite winter comes . . .

The closer I get to death, the more I love the earth, the thought
introduced itself as I sat shivering on my old park bench before
the dusk fog; as it has, I suppose, to every human being
who has ever lived
past forty.

A wingless, male, scared-looking angel of about sixteen—nobody wants to see that

Prow of my father's bald unbuilt house parting the stars

SEPTEMBER SUNFLOWER

Pale yellow light filled the room
I'd been lying in bed for a month
one afternoon

Yellow light filled the room
Don't let them get inside
your eyes, my evil
said
and lay their eggs there

Light filled the room

light I assumed
coming in through the window
but no

more a feeling, though light, too

a healing

And I saw again, September sunflower

petals intense yellow flames

child's drawing
of the sun

Ten feet tall blond
face

all pupil—

And loved again

And walked again

P.S.

I close my eyes and see
a seagull in the desert,
high, against unbearably blue sky.

There is hope in the past.

I'm writing to you
all the time, I am writing

with both hands,
day and night.

THE WORD "I"

Harder to breathe
near the summit, and harder

to remember
where you came from,

why you came

Winter's
harder, and harder to say
the word "I"
with a straight face,
and sleep—

who can sleep? Who has time

to prepare for the big day
when he will be required
to say goodbye to everyone, including
the aforementioned pronoun, relinquish
all earthly attachment
completely, and witness
the end of the world—

harder in other words
not to love it

not to love it so much

HOW YOU WILL KNOW ME

For days
like this, sepia
shades
a good coat

impermeable to the cold of this world, of a capaciousness to house that
which can only be named one's absolute and indivisible (unbeholdable
in its minuteness and hugeness) nonentity, before it is at last
unveiled

In my forty-eighth year, on the thirteenth day of the second month, as I
was wandering among the exiles along the river Charles under general
anesthesia, a small gray cross smudged on my forehead, the heavens
were opened, like a book, like an apple cut in half, and I saw I don't
remember what

Blizzard permitting
her ship should appear
about four in the morning
like a poet's
lonely fame.

THE NEW JERUSALEM

In the instant before sleep, I saw it
again: Earth
all water, all
ocean! Bathed
in this translucent blue ray, so gorgeous, like
Mary's—

And I knew again, for the millionth time, knew—
lying all alone there in the dark—you
can shut both your eyes
(you can pluck out your eyes), the light
will still be there

Rilke in one of his letters said Christ
is a pointing,
a finger pointing
at something, and we are like dogs
who keep barking and lunging
at the hand

Grave black grieving face in golden
space
above the sea
which is no more

That is,
which is not yet

QUEST

The bell which
when struck emits
silence—

I don't want to sleep with you
I want to wake up with you,

when I was sick in bed.

EPITAPH

Now I'm not the brightest
knife in the drawer, but
I know a couple things
about this life: poverty
silence, impermanence
discipline and mystery

The world is not illusory, we are

From crimson thread to toe tag

If you are not disturbed
there is something seriously wrong with you, I'm sorry

And I know who I am
I'll be a voice
coming from nowhere,

inside—

be glad for me.

THE POEM

It was like getting a love letter from a tree

Eyes closed forever to find you—

There *is* a life which
if I could have it
I would have chosen for myself from the beginning

DIARY OTHERWISE EMPTY

Caught a brown trout in a trickle of creek;

looks like rain.

When he is no longer needed Christ will come again.

ICON FROM CHILDHOOD

Bee light
The bees of the icon
The little prayer
to Mary, maybe
I won't remember
anything
only

the words. And
that these words
are only

things, but
that all things are shining

words, busy
silently
saying themselves—

they don't need
me.

THE NEW CHILD

The fish applaud the ocean;
I shake hands with the sky.
And there is this tall family
of trees I will visit, the water-
colored windows
of that ancient blue house
where I might have lived.

WALDEN

Sunlight and silence stood at a bend in the path suddenly;
wind moved, once, over the dark water
and I was back.
Far from the world of appearances,
the world of "gain and mirth."
So soon
there will be nobody

here going on
about death
and pain and change. No one here!
Spoking hallways of pines where the owl, eyes wide open, dreams—
there is a power that wants me to live, I don't know why.
Then I saw again
the turtle

like a massive haunted head
lumbering after the egg laying toward
the water and vanishing
into the water, slowly
soaring
in that element half underworld, half sky.
There is a power that wants me to love.

WALKING TO MARTHA'S VINEYARD

And the ocean smells like lilacs in late August—how
    is that.

The light there muted (silver) as remembered light.

Do you have any children?

No, lucky for them.

Bad things happen when you get hands, dolphin.

Can you tell us a little bit about your upbringing?

There is no down or up in space or in the womb.

If they'd stabbed me to death on the day I was born, it
    would have been an act of mercy.

Like the light the last room, the windowless room at the
    end, must look out on. Gold-tinged, blue

vapor trail breaking up now like the white line you see,
    after driving all day, when your eyes close;

vapor trail breaking up now between huge clouds resembling
    a kind of Mount Rushmore of your parents' faces.

And these untraveled windy back roads here—cotton
  leaves blowing past me, in the long blue
  horizontal light—

if I am on an island, how is it they go on forever.

This sky like an infinite tenderness, I have caught
  glimpses of that, often, so often, and never yet have
  I described it, I can't, somehow, I never will.

How is it that I didn't spend my whole life being happy, loving
  other human beings' faces.

And wave after wave, the ocean smells like lilacs in
  late August.

THE ONLY ANIMAL

The only animal that commits suicide
went for a walk in the park,
basked on a hard bench
in the first star,
traveled to the edge of space
in an armchair
while company quietly
talked, and abruptly
returned,
the room empty.

The only animal that cries
that takes off its clothes
and reports to the mirror, the one
and only animal
that brushes its own teeth—

Somewhere

the only animal that smokes a cigarette,
that lies down and flies backward in time,
that rises and walks to a book
and looks up a word
heard the telephone ringing
in the darkness downstairs and decided
to answer no more.

And I understand,
too well: how many times
have I made the decision to dwell
from now on
in the hour of my death
(the space I took up here
scarlessly closing like water)
and said I'm never coming back,
and yet

this morning
I stood once again
in this world, the garden
ark and vacant
tomb of what
I can't imagine,
between twin eternities,
some sort of wings,
more or less equidistantly
exiled from both,
hovering in the dreaming called
being awake, where
You gave me
in secret one thing
to perceive, the
tall blue starry

strangeness of being
here at all.

You gave us each in secret something to perceive.

Furless now, upright, My banished
and experimental
child

You said, though your own heart condemn you

I do not condemn you.

ACKNOWLEDGMENTS

The author wishes to thank the editors of the following journals, where some of these poems first appeared: *Can we have our ball back, Field, Gulf Coast, Long Shot, nowCulture, Perihelion, Salmagundi,* and *Slope.*

Special thanks to the editors of *The New Yorker,* where the following poems first appeared: "Cloudless Snowfall," "The Word 'I,'" "April Orchard," "Flight," "Year One," "Walking to Martha's Vineyard," and "The Only Animal." A number of these poems, sometimes in earlier versions, also appeared in two chapbooks: *God While Creating the Birds Sees Adam in His Thoughts* (Halfmoon Bay Press, Kalamazoo, MI) and *Hell & Other Poems* (Stride Books, UK).

The author also wishes to thank Jordy, Linda, Max, and Holly Powers, who opened their home to him during a hard time.

ABOUT THE AUTHOR

Franz Wright was born in Vienna in 1953 and grew up in the Northwest, the Midwest, and northern California. His most recent works include *The Beforelife* (which was a finalist for the Pulitzer Prize) and *Ill Lit: Selected & New Poems.* He has been the recipient of two National Endowment for the Arts grants, a Guggenheim Fellowship, a Whiting Fellowship, and the PEN/Voelcker Award for Poetry, among other honors. He works at the Edinburg Center for Mental Health and the Center for Grieving Children and Teenagers and lives in Waltham, Massachusetts, with his wife, Elizabeth.

A NOTE ON THE TYPE

This book was set in a modern adaptation of a type designed by the first William Caslon (1692–1766). The Caslon face, an artistic, easily read type, has enjoyed over two centuries of popularity in our own country. It is of interest to note that the first copies of the Declaration of Independence and the first paper currency distributed to the citizens of the newborn nation were printed in this typeface.